O9-BUB-238

EYE VOLTAGE

EYE VOLTAGE

A STONER'S BOOK OF 40 MIND-BLOWING OPTICAL ILLUSIONS

DR. SEYMOUR KINDBUD

AND THE MAUI WOWIE OPTICAL FACTORY

CIDER MILL PRESS

BOOK PUBLISHERS

© 2012 by Appleseed Press Book Publishers

This is an officially licensed book by Cider Mill Press Book Publishers LLC.

All rights reserved under the Pan-American and International Copyright Conventions.

No part of this book may be reproduced in whole or in part, scanned, photocopied, recorded, distributed in any printed or electronic form, or reproduced in any manner whatsoever, or by any information storage and retrieval system now known or hereafter invented, without express written permission of the publisher, except in the case of brief quotations embodied in critical articles and reviews.

The scanning, uploading, and distribution of this book via the Internet or via any other means without permission of the publisher is illegal and punishable by law. Please support authors' rights, and do not participate in or encourage piracy of copyrighted materials.

13-Digit ISBN: 978-1604332674
10-Digit ISBN: 1604332670

This book may be ordered by mail from the publisher. Please include $3.95 for postage and handling.

Please support your local bookseller first!

Books published by Cider Mill Press Book Publishers are available at special discounts for bulk purchases in the United States by corporations, institutions, and other organizations. For more information, please contact the publisher.

Cider Mill Press Book Publishers
"Where good books are ready for press"

12 Port Farm Road
Kennebunkport, Maine 04046

Visit us on the web!
www.cidermillpress.com

Text & Design: Tilman Reitzle
Book title: Courtney Edmands
Eagle eyes: Amy Paradysz

Printed in China

1 2 3 4 5 6 7 8 9 0

First Edition

IMAGE CREDITS: Vlue/Shutterstock: cover, back cover, 3, 6 (dude); Lukiyanova Natalia/frenta: cover, back cover, 3, 6, 40–41 (pattern); David Dohnal/Shutterstock: 4, 5, 7, 96 (seed); Hans Holbein, the Younger: 9 (*The Ambassadors*, 1533); Tilman Reitzle: 13, 17, 21, 23, 27, 38–39, 43, 45, 47, 49, 51, 94; Bojanovic/Shutterstock: 24–25 (surfer); EpicStockMedia: 24–25 (wave); Barry Barnes/Shutterstock: 29; vermicule/Shutterstock: 15, 31; Mark Grenier/Shutterstock: front flap, 26, 33, 35, 37; Danny Smythe/Shutterstock: 41 (stereoscope); NASA: 53; Library of Congress: 55; Marcel Clemens/Shutterstock: 57; Betacam-SP/Shutterstock: 58–59, 71; apdesign/Shutterstock: 61; VectoriX/Shutterstock: 63; Paul Fleet/Shutterstock: 65; Paul Prescott/Shutterstock: 66–67; Luis Stortini Sabor aka cvadrat: 68–69; Oleg Zhevelev/Shutterstock: 73; Joan Ramon Mendo Escoda/Shutterstock: 74–75; piotrwzk/Shutterstock: 76–77 (Vatican); vpix/Shutterstock: 78–79 (Rila, Bulgaria); Thomas Barrat/Shutterstock: 80–81 (*Short Cut*, 2003, by Elmgreen and Dragset); Alvaro German Vilela: 82–83 (Madrid); Cora Reed/Shutterstock: 84–85; stocker1970/ Shutterstock: 86–87 (M4 near London); valentina1988/Shutterstock: 88–89; supachart/Shutterstock: 90–91 (Lake Matheson); idreamphoto/Shutterstock: 93; shankz/Shutterstock: 94 (hand); casejustin/Shutterstock: back cover, flaps, 1, 4–5, 10–11, 75, 76, 81, 83, 96

CONTENTS

LIKE... INTRODUCTION

Welcome to this most awesome book! We've gathered here for you some of the most mind-boggling optical illusions we could legally include in a single volume. Originally we were going to tell you all about the very brainiac science that is behind the phenomena you will encounter in this book—things like the Hermann grid effect, contrast through contour enhancement, segregation of objects and background motion in the retina, complementary color juxtapositions, scintillating grids, psychology and visual perception, motion-based stabilization of vision, anomaly in the perception of rigid motion for limited spatial frequencies and angles, the concept of objectivity in relation to visual motion illusions, and the research done on lightness perception in cognitive neuroscience. But we figured that even just listing these things would have you drift off into space by the time we got to "Hermann grid."

So we skipped all that and will leave you with a simple warning: Do not read this book while driving a car, operating heavy machinery, or while under the influence of evil thoughts! Remember, if you go cross-eyed trying to see the stereo images, don't go too hard on yourself. Just chill. And enjoy.

SHAPES OF THINGS

This reproduction of a painting by Hans Holbein, Jr. shows two ambassadors to the court of, uh, the royal empire of... somewhere. This is where it gets interesting: Mr. Holbein decides to paint this freaky, long shape... *right on top* of this very awesome portrait.

As if that weren't enough, the only way to identify the shape is to hang this very large painting about umpteen feet up on some huge castle wall and then stand off way to the side underneath and crane your neck. *R-r-right.*

We'll save you the hassle. Turn the book about forty-five degrees and tilt... until you see... the shape. Whoa.

I know what you're thinking:
Dude, that is so *anamorphic.*

8

CHAPTER ONE

...in which literary obfuscation in the form of oblique introductory text communication gives way to a series of classic two-dimensional graphic explorations—utilizing the powers of complementary colors, concentric circles, and implied perspective—capable of inducing in the viewer a high degree of psycho-optical conundrum and mind-altering phenomena. In other words, get ready for the graphic world of...

PARALLEL UNIVERSE

Yes, you saw this in a book when you were a kid.
But, guess what. It's *still* freaky.

You say, No way those gray, horizontal lines are parallel!
And I'm like, Dude, they are *totally* and *utterly* parallel.

None more parallel, in fact.

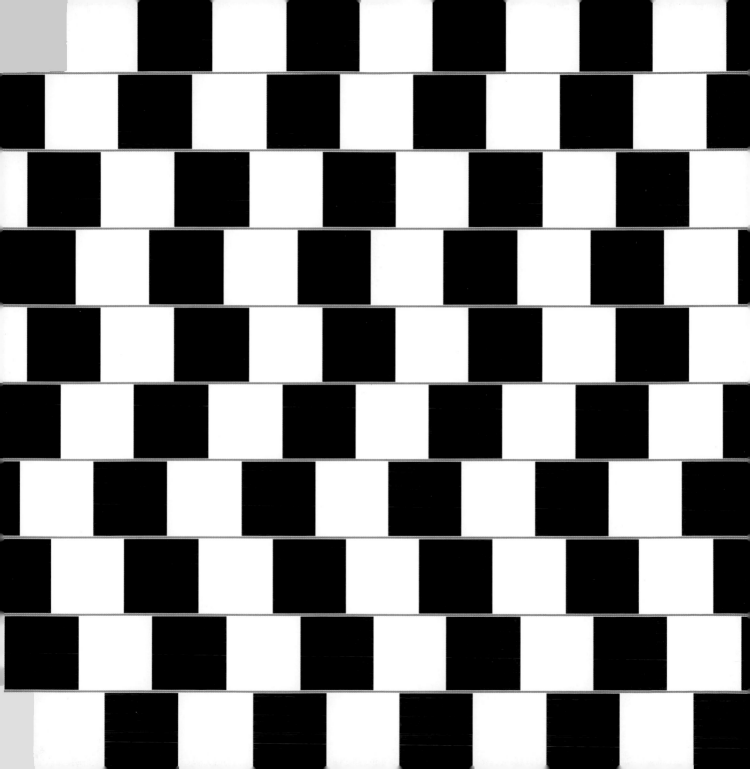

VERTICAL VERTIGO

So, dude. I know just what you're going to say:
   "These key-lime-pie-green lines cannot be
vertical. They are leaning *left*."
   And I'm like, Think again. They are *so*.
Completely. Amazingly. *Vertical*.

   By the way—did you say Key Lime Pie?
Du-u-u-de.
   Now you're talking.

SEEING SPOTS?

Take a look at the black dots on the opposite page. (Yes, those dots sitting squarely in the middle of where the gray lines intersect). Notice how they turn *white* when you're not looking at them?

Don't panic, dude. There is no need to call a doctor. They* say it's perfectly natural.

* This statement has not been evaluated by the FDA and should not be taken as an official medical diagnosis, advice, endorsement of any particular remedy, or like, uh, whatever. And who are those "they" we keep hearing about? Have they even seen this book? Dude.

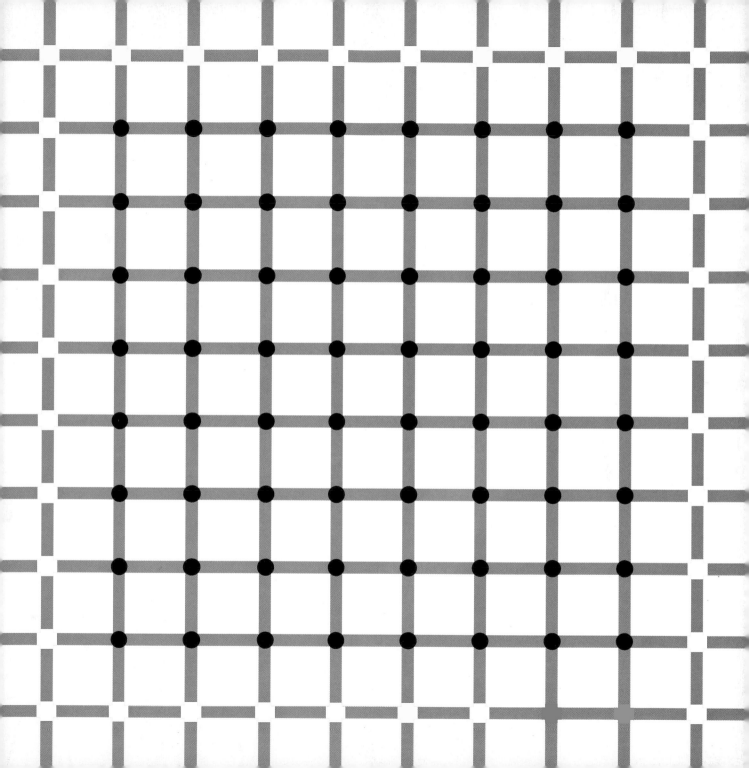

PINCH ME, I'M SEEING THINGS

Look closely at the black box in the middle of the facing page. Its edges appear to curve, as if being pinched by an unseen, mysterious force. However, I assure you that it's not under the influence of any edge-bending devices, or gratuitous magnetic disturbances. The edges of the box are perfectly, utterly, and completely *straight*. At this very moment. Just like *you*.

DIAMONDS ARE WHATEVER

If I told you that every one of these diamond shapes is the *exact same size and color*, would you believe me? You just might not. But check this out: they... *are*.

Here's how you can find out. If you're in the bookstore, open another copy of this book to the same page. (Don't ruin the book doing it, 'cause then you'll have to buy both copies. Which, like, wouldn't be bad for the publisher, but it might cut into your stash allowance to buy two copies.) Where was I?

Yes, so you overlap the two pages and move the diamonds near each other. Line up the top row of diamonds with the bottom row in the other book. You'll see that they totally *match*.

And you'll be, like, *"du-u-u-u-de!"*

STAIN REMOVER

See the fuzzy gray haze around the black dot in the center of the opposite page? (Yes, it's really there.) Now fix your stare squarely on the black dot.

Concentrate deeply on it for a few seconds. Then watch as the gray haze... completely *disappears*.

I agree. Everything in life should be this easy.

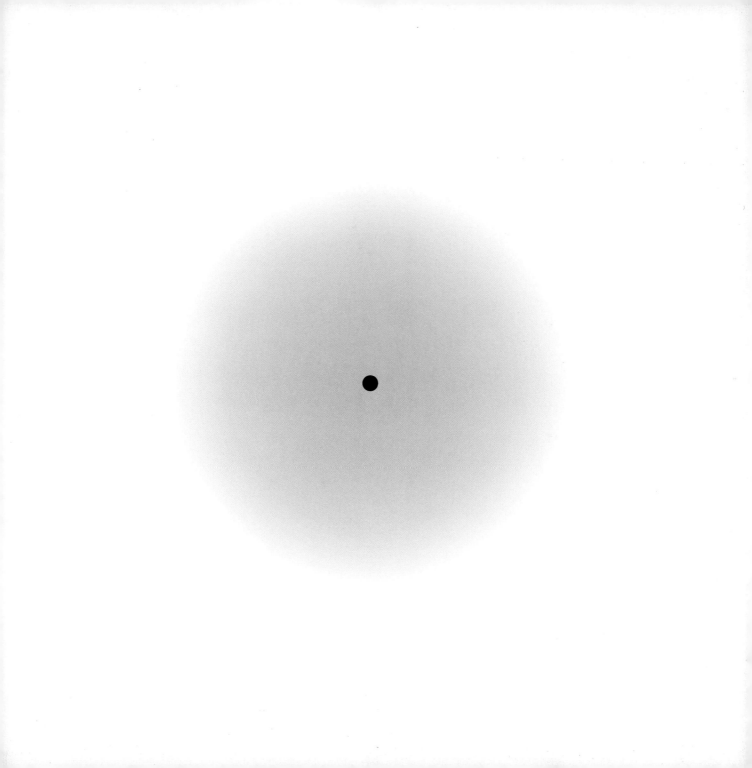

WIPEOUT?

These surfer chicks are pretty steady on their boards. So the only thing getting wiped out here might be your *illusions*, dude. In case you had any doubts: all of these three surfin' ladies are *exactly* the same size. How's that for perspective?

CHAPTER TWO

Wherein what is about to transpire is that two dimensions conspire to inspire... while you perspire. Whatever the next pages are content to do to you and your mind, the one thing they won't do is *stand still.*

Watch as the images on the following pages transport you straight into the heart of the metaphysical *spin cycle*. Get ready, it's time to do the...

BIG WHEELS KEEP ON TURNIN'

I know. You're thinking, man, that's *strong* herb—I'm seeing those ferris wheels *turning*! Before you jump to conclusionary statements about the qualitational merits of your herb, let me tell you that even your pals in the room who *haven't* had a toke may tell you *they're seeing it, too*.

Now if they say the wheel's turning *counter-clockwise*, however, keep an eye on them. They may be smoking some *really* wacked out stuff...

WAVELENGTH

While keeping your eyes fixed on the pattern on the opposite page, slowly move your head back and forth until you see... the *waves*.

Whatever you do, resist the impulse to wave *back*. At least, if you're enjoying this book in public and you like to *blend in*.

YOU'VE GOT THE MOTION

View the image on the facing page under a bright reading lamp and you just may find it... *pulsating*.

That's right my friend. Let the Doctor explain what's going on here. There's this scientific phenomenon that occurs when, you know, colors *vibrate*... because they *complement* each other.

"Hey Orange, you lookin' good tonight."

"Right back atcha, my Blue friend."

See? That's when stuff starts to *move*.

UNDER EXPANSION

Stay tuned for more stuff as soon as we're, like, done *expanding*. Until that time there is no need to read further. Everything of interest on this spread is happening on the opposite page. Seriously. Don't read any more of this text. Words simply don't suffice. Just look at the picture.

And just in case you're thinking, That's pretty expansive—how can I possibly *afford* it?

No worries, dude. This one's on the house.

SPIRAL ARCHITECT

Look at the white spot in the center of any of the four spirals on the facing page. Then shift your gaze to another white spot and notice how that spiral freezes right up . . . while the others start to *spin*.

It's like in those movies where a dude is pretending to be a statue in a museum. And then, like, another guy is walking through the place looking for the dude—the guy pretending to be the *statue*. And, as soon as the other guy *looks* at the statue, it stands perfectly *still*. You know, to evade capture and stuff.

Makes you wonder, eh?

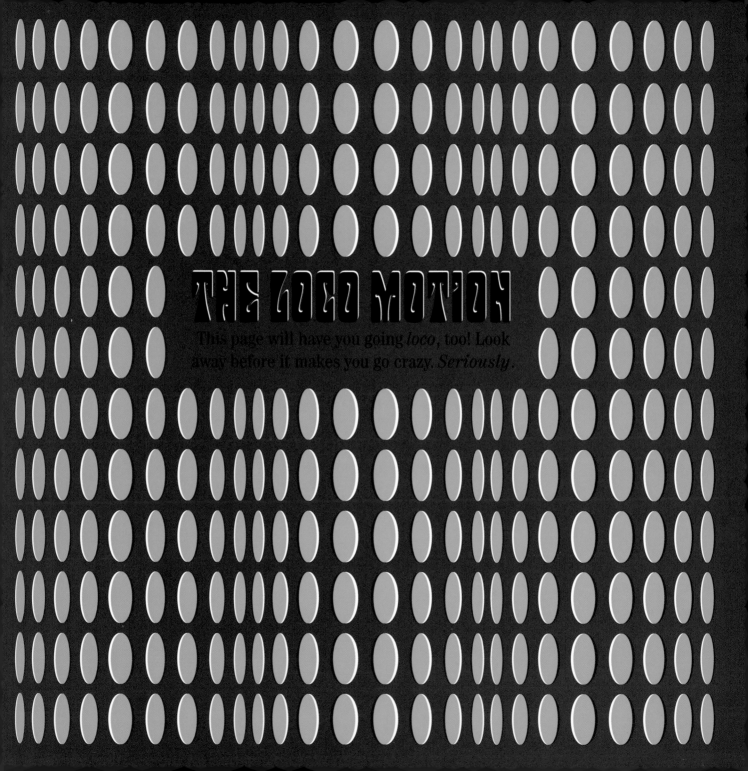

THE LOCO MOTION

This page will have you going *loco*, too! Look away before it makes you go crazy. *Seriously*.

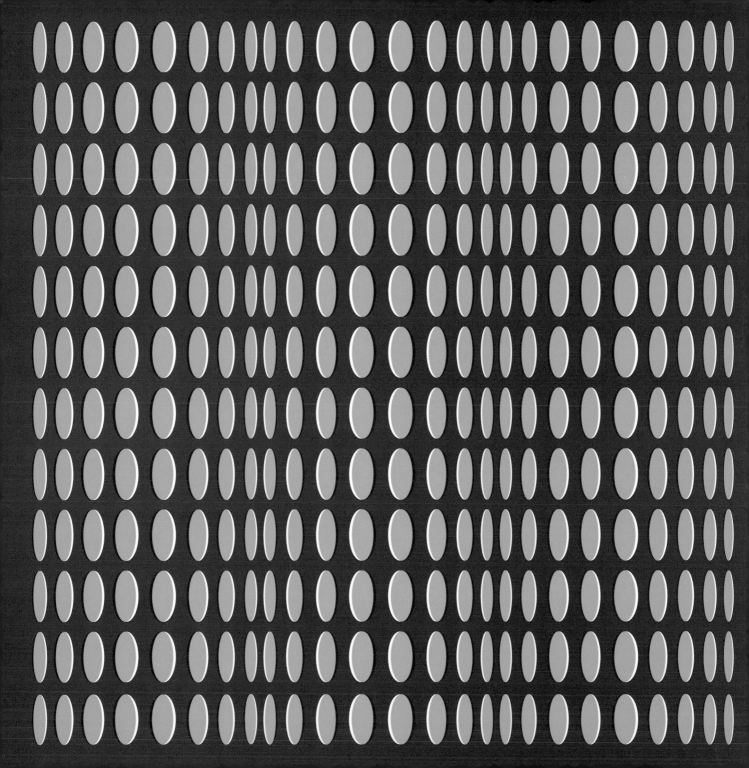

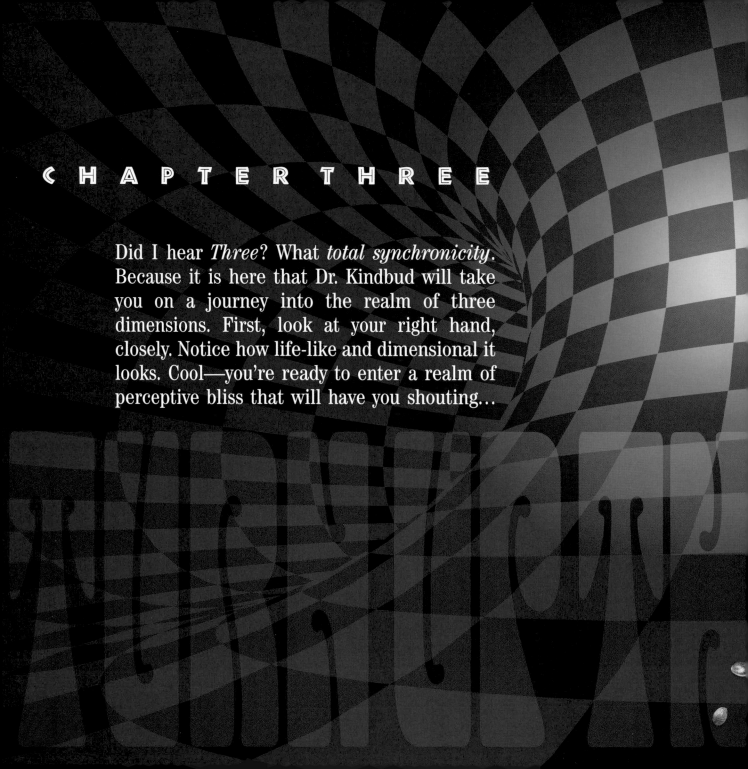

CHAPTER THREE

Did I hear *Three*? What *total synchronicity*. Because it is here that Dr. Kindbud will take you on a journey into the realm of three dimensions. First, look at your right hand, closely. Notice how life-like and dimensional it looks. Cool—you're ready to enter a realm of perceptive bliss that will have you shouting…

HOODOO YOU LOVE?

Brace yourself for some Bryce, dude. Relax your eyes and the hoodoos'll come right out at you. That's not voodoo or doodoo—it's *hoodoo*. These things are highly erotic, uh, I mean eroded. You know, when wind eats away at stuff for thousands of years... or even millions. A long time, dude. Still can't see it in stereo? Relax some more. Pick out a detail—a rock or other distinct shape—then let your eyes go out of focus until you see each repeated in double. Then overlap the two in the middle and, voilá, you're way deep into some real depth.

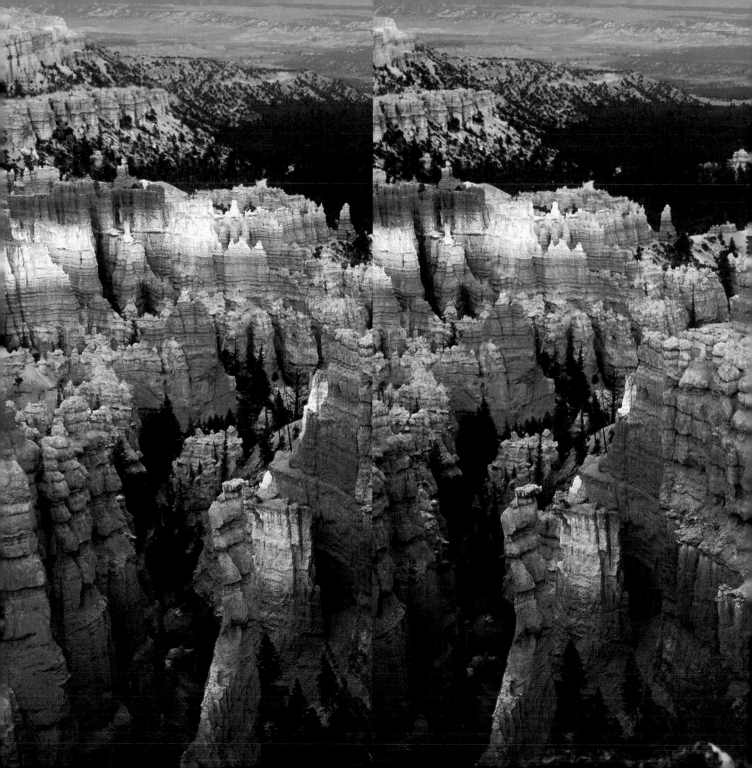

WALL OF HOODOO

Mwuah-ha-ha-ha!

LEAVES OF GRASS

A) The grass is always greener on the other side.
B) Green grass and high tides forever.
C) The green, green grass of home.
D) All of the above.

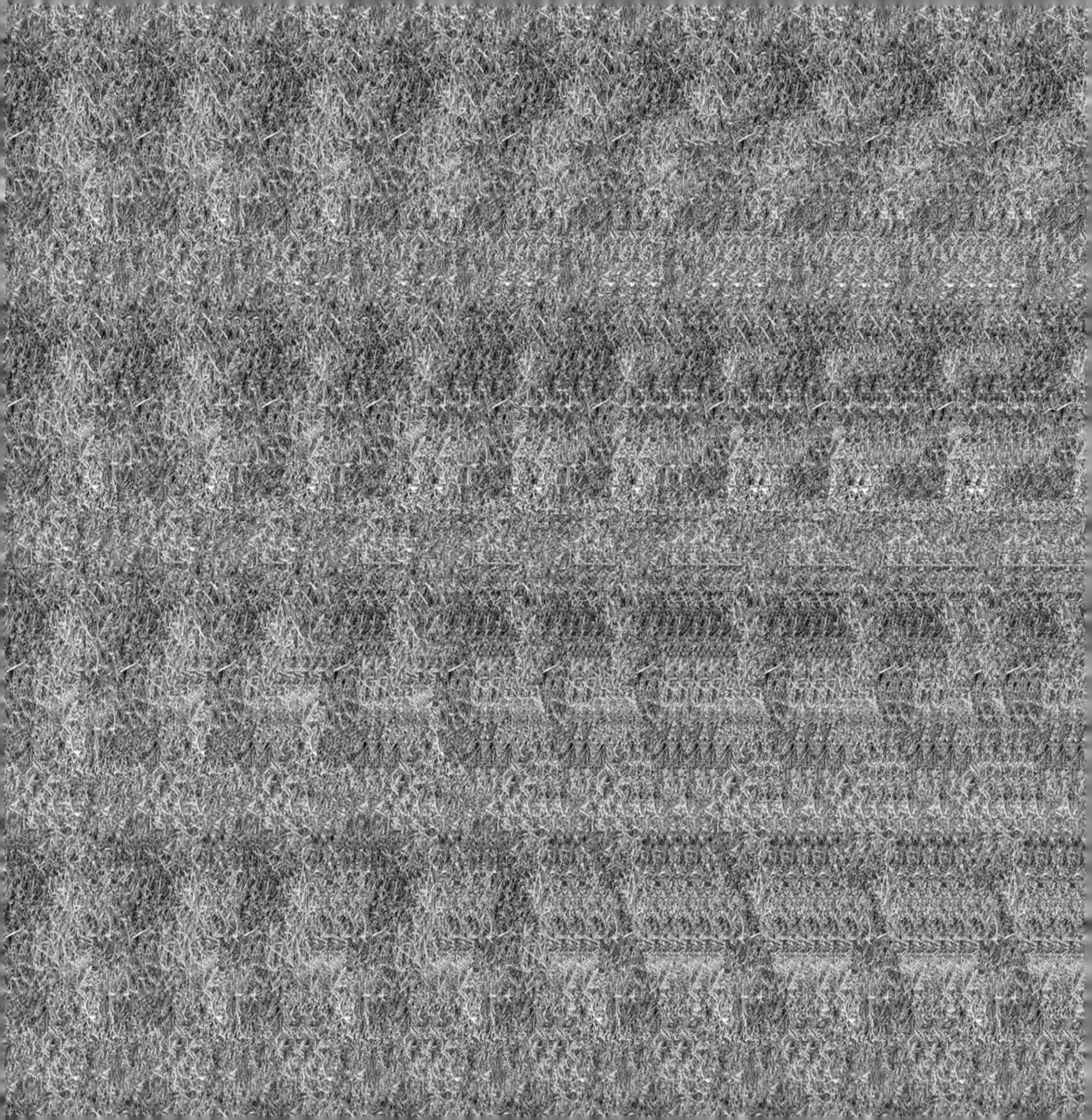

CANYONS OF THE MIND?

What mystery lurks in this unfathomable landscape
of gray matter, upon which thoughts are scattered like
rock across the mystic riverbeds of distant planets?

As you gaze upon this image, what thoughts erupt from
the the volcano of your mind? Thoughts of geological
cataclysm? Seismic pulsation? Outer space colonization?
Gemstone mining in Middle Earth?
Electron-microscope holography?

Or do you say to yourself,

Hey, it's time for...

...SOME POPCORN.

Du-u-u-u-de. Great minds think alike.

YOU ARE MY SUNSHINE

If we were in outer space (which we kind of *are*, depending on how you look at it) we'd be able to see the sun just like this. Except it would be way too bright to look directly at it. So it's a good thing NASA got some expensive gear to take this photo instead.

So you get to chill out, imagine yourself in a spacecraft orbiting the very center of our galaxy, and stare right at the sun. Because studies show—yes, Mama—that *is* where the fun is.

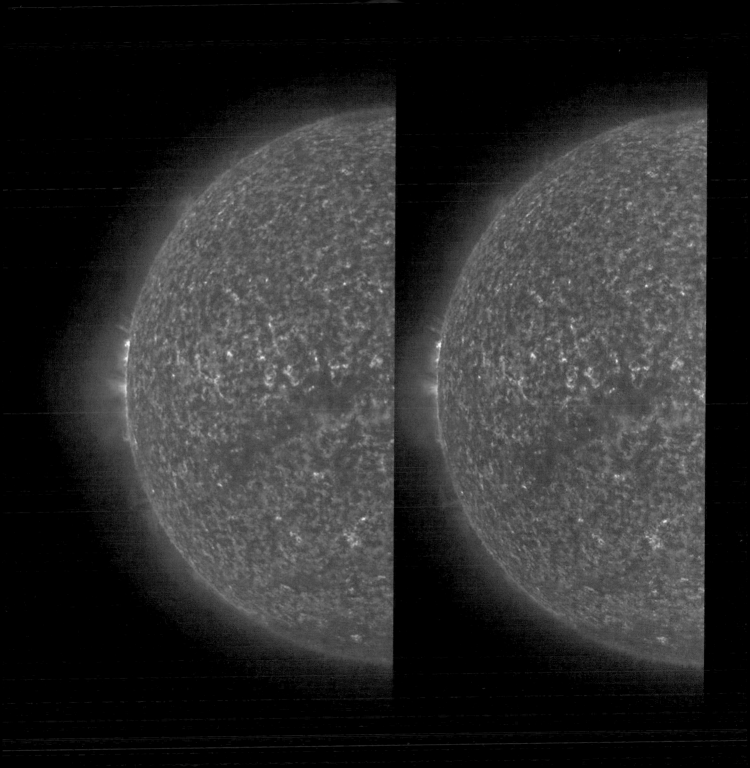

SPEECH!

Welcome back to earth, dude. How are you enjoying this proto-cosmo-dimensional time travel device called "a book" so far?

Are you ready for the next stop? Washington, D.C., March 4, 1905. You get the best seat in the house for the inaugural speech of President Teddy Roosevelt. We are *so. There.*

WE TWO ARE ONE

Totally.

IMPOSSIBLE

CHAPTER FOUR

Wherein that which cannot be built is constructed and we give thanks to the second dimension for kicking the third dimension's butt by visualizing... the fourth dimension, and marrying it with... uh... deep thoughts. It's that kind of chapter.

REALITY IS AN ILLUSION BROUGHT ON BY A LACK OF WEED

—Hey, didn't the dude from
Monty Python say that?

MY REALITY CHECK HAS BOUNCED AGAIN.

—Dude! They charge crazy fees for that.

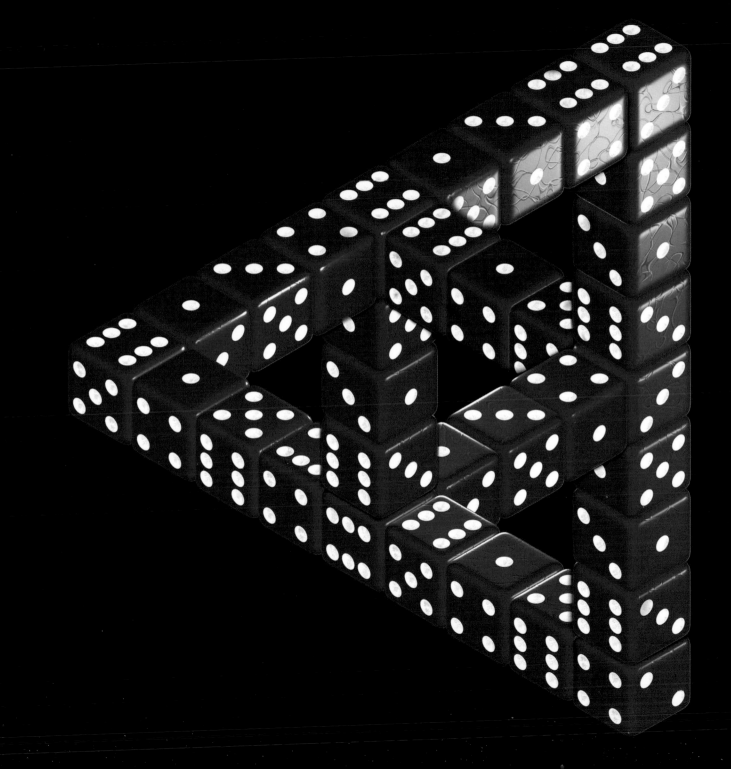

REALITY IS THE ILLUSION THAT JUST WON'T GO AWAY...

—Einstein just might have said that.

BULGE OR DENT?

—Your call, dude.

DEEP THOUGHTS

ARE REALLY, REALLY COOL...

...uh, if you can remember them.

BUILD IT AND THEY WILL COME

—I just felt like saying that.

CHAPTER FIVE

An illusion of an illusion. Is that a double negative (a big no-no) or is it *twice* the illusion?

Du-de. If you thought it was an illusion, but you are actually under the *illusion* that it's an illusion, then it's... *reality*.

And you might say, Get real! And I'm like, Dude... *exactly*.

So, in this chapter we'll look at things that really *should* be illusions but—for reasons known only to foreigners—*aren't*.

Look in a mirror,
and you see yourself.
Look in a bunch of mirrors,
and you see *infinity*....

Dude, I'm impressed
you'd actually bother to
hold this book up to a mirror
and see what it says.

Many churches in old Europe appear to have been designed to completely *mess with your mind.*

Dude, I don't mean the dogma, the dietary restrictions, or the holiday schedule—I'm only talking about... the *ceiling*.

In some cases, the *entire building* appears to be an optical illusion, like this monastery in Bulgaria. (Don't poke an eye out when you turn the book sideways!)

Europeans don't just paint their ceilings in trippy scenes. They also delight in messing with your mind when you're just innocently going to the courthouse, the library, or the art museum.

I ask you, in all earnestness:
What are these Europeans *on*?

Then again, we have Las Vegas.

THE MIRAGE

Put *that* in your pipe and smoke it.

Look, it's a giant art installation of
neon lights stretching for two miles!

Seriously, though—the truth is even more far out:
It's a photograph of *time travel*. This photo captured
a moment that happened long ago, combined
with one that happened *even longer* ago,
and a nearly *infinite* number
of moments in between.
Dude, *infinite*.

Welcome to the great outdoors... uh... indoors!

How long did it take you to realize this image...

...is upside down?

FIND THE ILLUSION

Now that you're thoroughly trained in viewing optical illusions, the time has come to see how your experience of this book has fine-tuned your viewing skills.

Closely study the image on the facing page. Notice the silhouettes, the reflection of the sunlight. Note the camera angle, the horizon line. You may ask yourself, Is that a one-point or two-point perspective? You may note the interplay of positive and negative space and venture to find the hidden image among the shapes created by the two.

And you may, after thorough study, conclude that there are no optical illusions at all—that *it's a gratuitous image of a gorgeous chick with a surfboard on a beach at sunset.*

And, dude—you're absolutely correct.

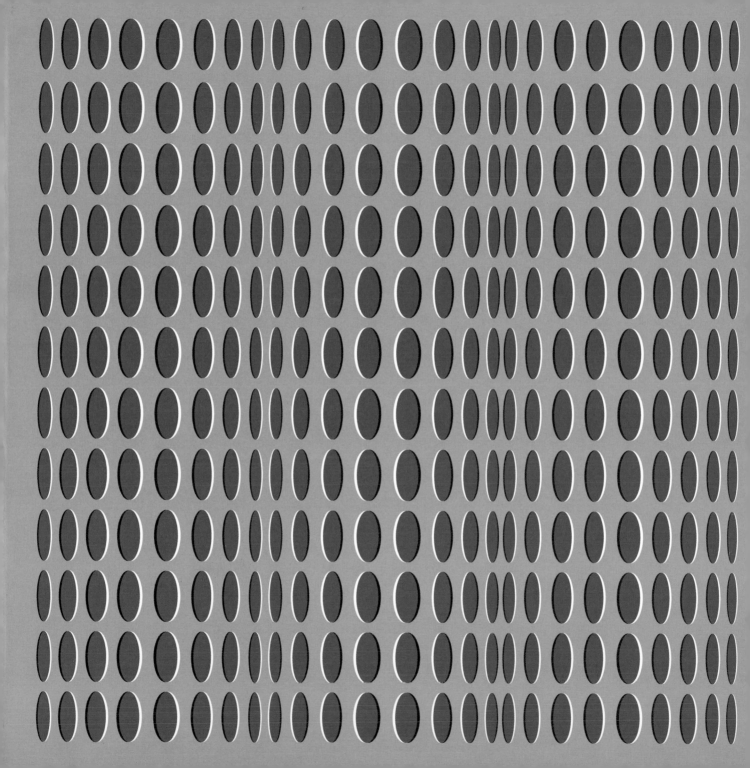

ABOUT CIDER MILL PRESS BOOK PUBLISHERS

Good ideas ripen with time. From seed to harvest, Cider Mill Press
brings fine reading, information, and entertainment together between
the covers of its creatively crafted books. Our Cider Mill bears fruit
twice a year, publishing a new crop of titles each spring and fall.

Visit us on the Web at
www.cidermillpress.com

or write to us at

12 Port Farm Road
Kennebunkport, Maine 04046

CIDER MILL
PRESS

BOOK
PUBLISHERS